LAND

RUTH BIDGOOD

CinnamonPress
INDEPENDENT INNOVATIVE INTERNATIONAL

Published by Cinnamon Press
Meirion House
Tanygrisiau
Blaenau Ffestiniog
Gwynedd, LL41 3SU
www.cinnamonpress.com

The right of Ruth Bidgood to be identified as author of this work has been asserted by her in accordance with the Copyright, Designs and Patent Act, 1988. Copyright © 2016 Ruth Bidgood
ISBN:978-1-910836-35-4
British Library Cataloguing in Publication Data. A CIP record for this book can be obtained from the British Library.

All rights reserved. No part of this publication may be reproduced, stored in a retrieval system, or transmitted in any form or by any means, electronic, mechanical, photocopying, recording or otherwise without the prior written permission of the publishers. This book may not be lent, hired out, resold or otherwise disposed of by way of trade in any form of binding or cover other than that in which it is published, without the prior consent of the publishers.

Designed and typeset in Palatino by Cinnamon Press. Printed in Poland.

Original cover design by Adam Craig © Adam Craig

Cinnamon Press is represented in the UK by Inpress Ltd and in Wales by the Welsh Books Council.

The publisher acknowledges the assistance of the Welsh Books Council.

Acknowledgements

Thanks to the following magazines, in which a number of these poems have appeared: *Agenda, Envoi, Interpreter's House, London Grip* (online), *New Welsh Review, Poetry Salzburg Review, Poetry Wales, Roundyhouse, Scintilla, Wales Arts Review* (online) *and to* The Ledbury Festival 20th Anniversary Anthology, in which 'Enigma' appears.

Contents

One Day	9
Land-music	10
Echo	11
The Stumpy Tree	12
Dark	13
Ghosts	
1. Ghosts	14
2. Tŷ Pwci	15
3. Epynt	16
4. From Time to Time	17
Desk-top	18
Gift Shop	19
The Bathroom	20
Handsome Piddock	21
The Giant Squid	22
Treasure	24
Hills	26
Walking in Moonlight	27
Swansea Angel	28
Twelve Days of Christmas	29
Dark River	30
Source	31
Parrot's Beak	32
The Preaching	34
Walk to the Rock	35
Scars	36
Undefined	37
Cadences	38
Dogs' Voices	39
Wrong Turn	40
Enigma	42
Triptych	
1. Portrait of a Devotee	43
2. Oswald's Well	44
3. The Yew	46
Now	47
Ambivalence	48
Truth	49

Gulls' Voices	50
White Bird Flying	51
The Lizard	52
Pheasants	53
Escapes	54
Toad in May	55
Dice Game on Dinas	56
Enjoy	57
The Ash-Tree	58
Sleepers	59
Country Church at Night	60
Landscape in Spring	61
Leaving for Home	
1	62
2	63
Reading Traherne	64
Moor at Dusk	65
Stones on the Moor	66
Limestone	67
Abundance	
1. Making May	68
2. The Golden Horse	69
3. Apricot Climate	70
4. Cider Mill	71
The Train	72
Verity	73
Lark Ascending	74
Waiting for the Tide	75
Happy Ending	76
Elms	77
Extremes	78
Encroachment	79
Defiance	80

To Anne Cluysenaar

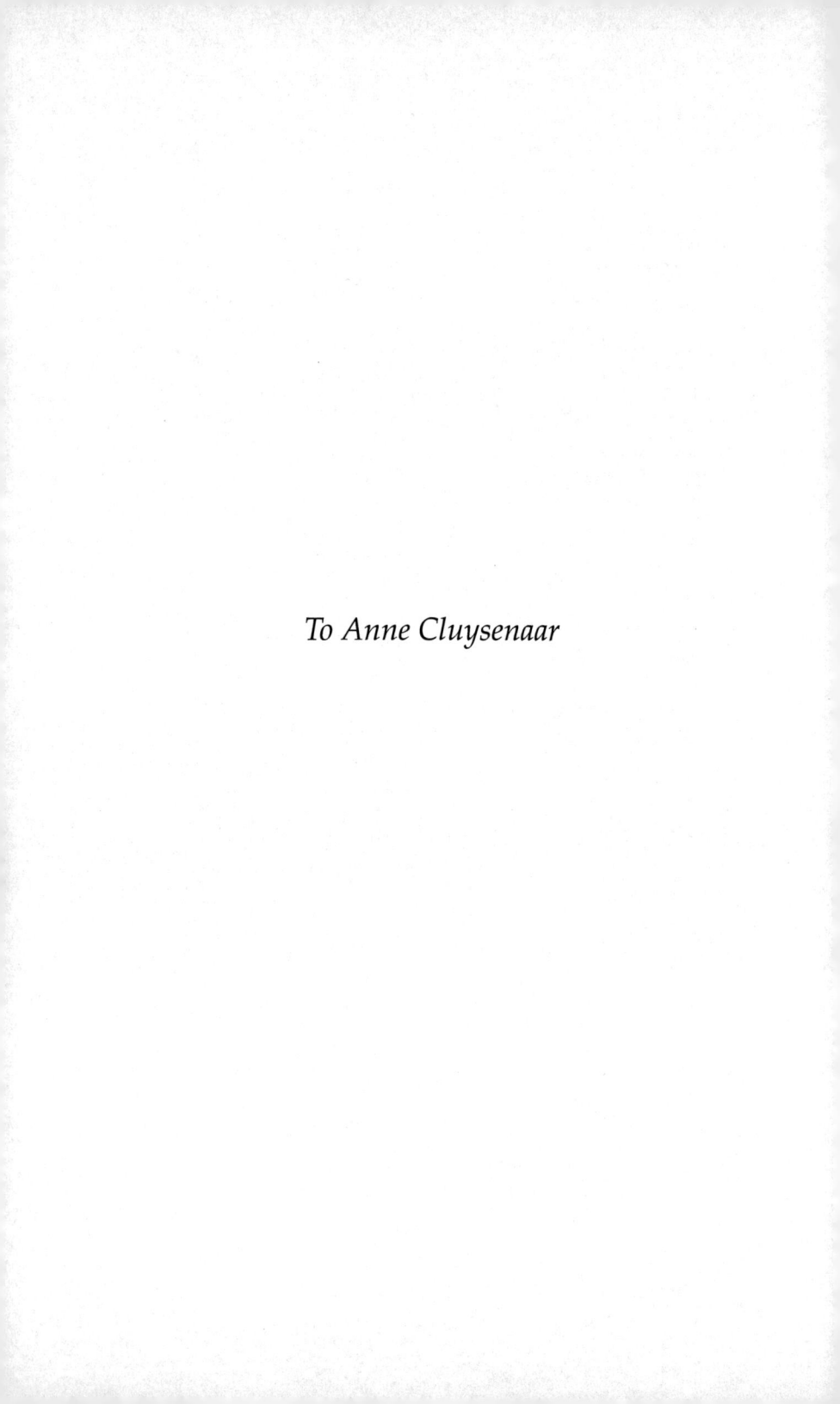

Land-Music

One Day

for Anne

Could death unmake
a day made so well?
I have not thought so.

Opening the album again, I see,
as it was then, the two of us, friends
not in the picture, but there, our eyes
delighting in what the camera saved,
surge of a field, promise of budded boughs,
line of hills beyond.

Over pub lunch there were stories
of your animals at home, of doves
you would write about. And lightly
ideas crossed the table, to and fro—a sharing
of your profundities, laughter, questions,
warmth, serenity. Something
was made, and would last.

It is with me now as we stand
out of frame, savouring
the brink of spring, perhaps both
having some notion of endlessness
hidden in a carefree day.

Land-music

After a wintry spring, heat and golden air.
Repetitive rhythm of larch-trunks,
downward-swooping phrases of branch,
admit moment by moment
brilliant notes of light
preluding the lake's full dazzle.

So long without a day like this!—
and now it's huge, inclusive, amazes
with the way it holds the far and near,
such tracts of time, so many acres
of loved known land, and yet such mystery.

Even the small dead paths no longer
debouching on our road—
the ones we walked, that now are wilderness
again, sealed off by prickly snarl of growth—
today make heard faint lasting songs.

And this man-made lake,
smoothing, formalising, changing
the flanking hills' proportions, sends out
into summer air, together
with chords of its own compulsion,
and soft glissandos from receding distance,
the notes of clefts and windings here,
drowned wooded crags, inescapable
harmonics of all we just remember.

Echo

Winter morning, early. High wind.
Drawn curtains; beyond,
thump, boom, drone, a distant crack.

My mind jumps back
to a still day of sun
in a bad summer. Pointing down
through tree-hung water,
my camera caught a shape,
a small blue submarine —
a carp, something not known
in that little lake.

Questions — how? when?
who had planned, perhaps,
to stock this hidden water?
what other dusky craft
were plying silently, shapes
refracted in quivering dimness? —
some setting out on small journeys
with a meaning known to them,
each move a mystery to me?

Stillness was broken by the crack
of a long-vulnerable branch,
falling just then, joining just now
with this chill day's havoc.

Early morning dark. High wind.
Drone, boom, crack.
Cool dimness below sun-darts
on the lake's surface. The branch
breaks and falls. Poised,
ready to vanish,
the blue shape of the carp.

The Stumpy Tree

Of all the January trees
rising black and stark at the roadside,
this one, stumpiest, clumsiest, challenges,
evoking a notion of the erroneous,
failed, grotesque.

Trunk shapelessly bulging, holding up
untidy swathes of ivy; top
distorted by remains of unskilled
pollarding, it spells
inadequacy, disappointment—

little humiliations, attempts
at giving help, when there were always
others who gave it better; love
breaking through thorns to reach
no wake-up kiss, but lukewarm liking.

Of all the black and naked trees
along the January road, this may seem
the one to match, involuntarily,
form to idea, claim kin,
catch at the heart.

Dark

If it weren't so dark
I could do wonders—
spot a shortcut
to jump the parallels,
reach a universe
that might seem home.

If it weren't so dark
I'd see my way
to rearrange time,
let coiling complexities
unwind and make
a sunlit road to joy.

If it weren't so dark
I'd see at last
pattern in those hints
of reachable elsewhere,
broken pictures that can't cohere—
if only it weren't so dark.

Ghosts

1. Ghosts

The pier, twin-turreted,
seemed to move as the sea moved,
with an uncertain undulation.
I remember far off a lighthouse,
but not precisely where, only
that it answered lights of the town
coming on at dusk. There was still
pink in the sky, and sharp colours
of houses along the coast.
I recall a touch of fantasy
in their lines, but in that halfway light
who knows?—and it was long ago.

What I am sure of is that this
was an embarkation point, and not
for a foreseen voyage, not
for a sure destination.
There were ghosts in that twilight, hungry
for departure, whose journey-dole
had never been paid.

If I remember and remember
is it too late? Can I learn how to pay,
how to be sure another ghost
is not still restlessly craving
to set out over unsteady sea
under darkening sky?

2. Tŷ Pwci

Why did it play such a trick?, she would ask,
old Hannah, sitting disconsolate
in the new shack her neighbours made.

Why did it burn my house?—I never
cursed it, never forgot the saucer of milk
at night, never the words at morning,
Pwci, quietly come in, pwci, quietly go.

I laughed at the frightened faces
of the servant-girls, filling their pails
at the spring, running, stumbling downhill,
spilling half the water, screeching
I saw the ghost! I saw the pwci!

Fools and liars!—it never showed itself.
It would come and go, and all I felt
was a breath of that wind we call
wind of the feet of the dead.

Yet it was no ghost of woman or man.
I couldn't call it friend. It was something
belonging to the hill. But why
did it play that trick on me, the pwci?

Why am I here, and the old life
gone in the flames?

3. Epynt

I can't remember the farms.
Forgive me, Cefn y Fedw, Cwm Car, Gwybedog,
all you other houses lost, you phantom fields.
Forgive me for my love of your supplanters,
moulded moorland stripped of husbandry,
narrow road unrolling toward a skyline
of the Beacons, never the same two journeys running,
black and sharp on turbulent sky, enigma glimpsed
through mist, or in high summer a golden promise.

I've read the story —
An army's demands, leaving enforced, false hints
that with war's end return might come.
Forgive me, Yscir Fawr, Cefn Bryn, Tir-bach,
that your ghosts trouble me so rarely,
that my eyes and ears are jarred so little
by today's few red flags, peremptory notices,
far-off manikins who might be playing at war.

Forgive me that what I meet
in these desolate miles is an austere
beauty, and almost always, peace.

4. From Time to Time

They say she's been seen, from time to time,
standing at an upstairs window.
No-one ever sees her clearly, yet
they are sure she's always gazing out
over that huge landscape I have loved
from the moment I first stood
by the rickety porch.
                      The faded house
looks as though once it just missed
a touch of grandeur. Many say it's a house
with 'something about it'.
                         It would always
have been lifted into specialness
by its view—that vast quiet expanse
of hills, dips, hills again, that stretches
beyond the window where she still
comes to stand, from which maybe
she sees a freedom she never knew.
Maybe she hopes it's even now
to be hers; or stands tortured by beauty,
the cruel salt in her still-open wounds.

I've never seen that enigmatic form, yet when
frustration or disappointment brings
a sadness out of all proportion;
or when illogical hope suddenly
expands the view from my heart, it's then
I picture her, then I remember how it is
to look out over first a gentle slope,
then a downward plunge to boskiness
of fields, a tawny climb to hilltop moors,
horizon mountains merging with mist,
and further, what that watcher surely seeks,
endless embracing of the craved unknown.

Desk-top

Every time I look, it's like touching.
The hills in my desk-top photograph
look warm behind a cool soft draggle
of thinning mist. One house on the slope
crouches by puff-ball bushes and a dark strong fir.
Below, there towers up a fan-shaped bank
of greyish trees; they seem fluffy, but can't be,
for this is February. Further away, more mist
surges from a hidden valley, into a realm
of indecision- cloud blurring hill-edges,
sky a sea whose islands may be outcrops,
a doubtful hint of high land beyond.

I am drawn back to the nearer slopes, the known
contours, recognising, perhaps, some limit
to this looking with love, feeling a need
for faithfulness to the specific, unique,
to something undeniably my own.

Gift Shop

Dismissively she ran her gaze
over the graded offerings in the gift shop,
rejecting little souvenirs ('tat', said her eyes),
summer handbags, even maps
and illustrated guides.
                                    For her
it was all irrelevance, let-down, after
the seemingly unpretentious dignity
of the old mansion: ample curve of river,
green flanking path: quirk
of red bridges in the water-garden:
column and bower: exuberance
of roses massed, enclosed.

I thought her wrong. The house
(ambivalent though my encounter
with it might be) I saw as doing
what it had always done—getting by,
giving itself the chance of another year,
another decade, maybe a century:
saving itself from rot and crash,
being still there, going on
uttering its unique word.

The Bathroom

My grandmother's terraced cottage
was halfway to modernity—
it had a bathroom, outside.

Opposite the back door,
across a dim covered way,
a windowless room with ceiling
of heavily clouded glass
made even sunlight murky,
dark weather menacing.

Yet I remember, not without pleasure,
the unique scent of its damp brick floor;
green echoes from the huge potted plant
whose name I never learned;
a whiff of rankness.

Grudgingly the bath-tap trickled out
warmish water tinged with rust.
I sat in the shallows, planning
small enterprises, forgotten for years now,
while the dank ambience that fostered them
I can still call up, wondering why it keeps
that perverse, disproportionate charm.

Handsome Piddock

With thanks to *British Shells*

The handsome Piddock sometimes has a shell
six inches long, creamy white,
beautiful. Yet its valves
cannot completely enclose
the ample proportions of the animal's
white body.
                The Piddock excavates
to hide itself. It rocks, it twists, but never
completely rotates, keeping its foot
firmly stuck to the burrow
and ejecting powdered rock
by spasmodic contractions
of long, stout, yellowish siphons.

At night it shows the bluish-white light
of its phosphorescence, intense
in warm summer dark, illumining
the mysterious depths of rock-pools
with points of light.

Thin-shelled and brittle-seeming,
yet hard, resistant, stone-borer,
the beautiful one, this is the Piddock,
the handsome Piddock.

The Giant Squid

Locked away in lethal pressures,
irredeemable dark,
the embodiment of a sick mind's
nightmare? Or real,
no Kraken of fantasy?

The TV screen comes alive
with smiling excited scientists, depth-bound.
Reaching out from the screen
is the passionate hope
of seeing at last a creature
half-legendary, wholly wanted, long sought for.

Watching, I'm conscious
of the crushing pressure above, around
the small vulnerable vessel.
Yet those in it, sinking deeper
into dark, seem to have no such thoughts,
only the thrill of catching a glimpse,
amid limitless black, of beings
unrecognised, outlined
in self-engendered light.

At last, triumphant cries!
There, filling the screen,
is the Giant Squid, monstrous
in size only, self-lit, soft-lit,
gleaming gold. For a brief time
blackness is only a foil
for this shining. Even
the great tentacles move not to clutch,
not now, but delicately,
frondily, overlapping, draping,
sliding, circling, waving
in elegant passages of dance.

Suddenly it contracts, recedes, is gone.
A few lesser creatures shine
at the screen's edge, then once more
there's the unbroken dark.

Treasure

Two pre-Raphaelite girls,
one mirroring the other,
droop naked-shouldered
on tiles each side of the fire.

They are not mermaids,
yet their flimsy gowns
spread past hidden feet
into fish-tail shapes.

Their gentle passivity
seems to provoke
little flames of gas
into leaping gestures
over glowing coals.

Outside, a windy tumult
of roof-tops, trees, hill after hill,
churns darkly into distance
under insistent clouds.

Huge, beautiful in gloom,
demanding, the view
drags me back and back
to the window.
                Yet, leaving,
my last, most searching look,
that stores the day's chief treasure,
is at the wistful drooping heads,
pallid shoulders of the fireside girls.

It is as if their sheer
incongruity, in this house
perched on a shelf above
such stormy grandeur,
spells the unpredictability
of beauty's manifestations,

dares me, confronted with dark
majesty, horizon-wide, to accept
a minor man-made elegance,
and greet its little prettiness with love.

Hills

Teatime. The hotel
buzzed gently with chat,
chinked with spoons, flowed
from a score of spouts.
Out of the window, rooftops,
glimpses of gardens, dusty gleams
of sun on cars. Beyond, hazy hills.

How restful it seemed, not
to feel much about anything—
to sink into smooth folds
of the soft-spoken room, lazy warmth
of an unemphatic townscape.

Yet though that day the distant hills,
hovering half-asleep, withheld
their darkness and their ecstasies,
the sense of them could still destroy
sleek artificial calm, bring back
tumult, rough abrasion, joy.

Walking in Moonlight

'Dirty old town, dirty old town' — the song reminds me
of our walk, with moonlight never so bright
on sullied scruffiness, the streets of home. My mind
skimmed forward to unbelievable old age,
to looking back. And here it is, just as I thought,
or nothing like it.
                      Here am I, having leapt
so many chasms, clawed back up from some,
sauntered or struggled along so many roads,
stony, slushy, grassy-smooth, crazily steep,
finding nothing as unexpected as the loves
along the way, nothing as predictable
as tonight, this moonlight, this magical
sameness, this surprise, back again, everlasting.

Swansea Angel

photograph by Bernard Mitchell

A winged head, this angel.
Short layered wings at the temples,
hair braided above. A woman's face,
eyes blank—one can choose
to see them shut, or gazing
on mysteries out of view.

The angel is bodiless, it seems—
winged head, seat of the soul,
of wisdom, dominion. Yet
she is fertile, rich with the future.
Surely she dreams her invisible
beautiful body. Her mouth dreams a kiss.

Twelve Days of Christmas

Tonight I've escaped
tinsel December and the clinging ghost
of childhood's candle-dark morning.
Lord of Misrule, King of the Bean,
I know his domain—twelve days
of ambivalence and power,
when the dead live, and chaos
drums through the dark.
The impossible is warm in my arms.
Through torchlit hours, dusk at noon,
twelve days dance; joy
is believable, joy is now.

Dark River

Walking up from the village.
I caught sight, at the bridge ahead,
of a dark patch in the roadway,
unexplained blackness on grey,
and found a few feet of no-road,
a child-sized plunge to the river below.

Easy to see how a timber-lorry, overweening,
massively stacked with poles, could have ripped
the meagre road-skin from this track, made to bring
the Victorian faithful to their new church,
and strip the faithless of their excuses.
                                       Now could be seen
the river's otherness, as imperturbably
it flowed on, seeming to assert
alien identity.
                    The familiar view
from the bridge-rails had shown it
linked calmly with people—
their stream, their meadow,
their local bit of surviving pastoral.
But this water, swifter than I had realised,
dark under the penetrated road,
was an unplanned reminder
of the primitive, uncontrollable—
perhaps after all not alien, but kin
to dark of the heart.

Source

The map shows boggy land
above old fields. Conventional symbols,
rushy pincushions, warn of slushy stumbling.
An irregular line of infant river
dwindles towards the source.
This can be anti-climax.
                       I remember once,
after long following, backwards and up,
of calm full river, clattering stream,
peaty brook, I came at last
to a damp patch between
molinia clumps. Singularly
lacking in drama, it had nothing
to suggest the start of anything
vital, any upspring of primal life.
It might well have been
a dispirited ending, a seeping-away.

But staring at it, bent on finding
something to salvage from what was meant
to be adventure, I saw a small
upswelling of moisture, a merging
of drops from one wispy stalk
with drops from another. There,
under thin draggled grasses,
was the tiny beginning of a flow.

This, after all, did seem like life,
whose promises aren't always obvious,
whose glories can hide within
an unlikely first draft.
Into the minuscule trickle
I dipped my fingers crossed.

Parrot's Beak

Parrot's Beak? Not a name
I believed, at first, for a few
outlying acres of conifers, part
of a forest called after the ruin
it had swallowed—Cluniau.

For centuries, we have been naming
hills, rocks, pools, bogs, fields—
first, no doubt, in the lost
languages of dawn: then Welsh:
then English.

          Cors yr Hwch, Bog of the Sow.
Drum Da Gwylltion, Hill of Wild Cattle.
Devil's Staircase, Wolf's Leap.
Cae Kaiser (said like a stutter), the Kaiser's Field.
Horne's Ley—he farmed here a while,
then left; a few decades on
is hardly remembered—but his name stays.

Now, Parrot's Beak? So near
the wild ancientness of source-land,
where the Welsh names are all of darkness—
Banc Du, Black Hill: Creigiau Duon, Black Rocks:
Chwarel Du, Black Quarry: where winter seems
the only natural season, where ice rules,
an ever-present frisson in the mind
even in months of sun.

Parrot's Beak? Why this
hint of the exotic, this touch
of comedy? I was shown on a map
the forest, that was thought one day
and seen thus ever after, to be
parrot-shaped ('more like a chicken',
said one), with a pert curved beak.

I am absorbing the name,
seeing its nowness dissolve
into permanence, inappropriateness
into the acceptable—spontaneous,
probably lasting, a flash of strange colour
lighting dark of the blaenau, becoming
true neighbour, heading for its own
ancientness, unplanned harmony.

The Preaching

Summer. Firs rank on rank
make a heaviness on the hill.
The path plods on through dark,
still and close, oppressed
by excessive sun outside,
and stabbed now and then
by a knife of light.

Here was bare hill when once in summer
a woman wearily trudged this path
to the village downstream, for the preaching—
driven by longing for the unflinching words,
majestic assurance of the Calvinist,
incantatory voice, monitory forefinger
injecting certainties into the very air.

Hereabouts she fell. A heaviness
must have weighed her down, the tired plodding
made her heart miss its beat one last time.
A knife of hot light struck through her,
then there was dark.   She lay on the path
with her arms stretched forward, as if
she knew something must be grasped,
held to.   More rigid than dragooned trees,
with its own darkness of inflexible
judgement, piercing blade
of condemnation, the heady message
of the man she had craved to hear
may have filled her as she fell. Yet
her outstretched arms were reaching
for more of mercy, perhaps, than he ever knew.

Summer again, Heaviness in the trees,
weariness on the path. Now and then,
fleetingly, breaking the dark,
a sharp intuition of light.

Walk to the Rock

When he was eight
we went to the Rock of the Birds.
He was ahead of us, eager
to get his first sight of the Rock.
When we reached the forest gate, and met
the openness of afternoon light
over green and tawny solitudes
of the upper valley, he stopped,
eyes fixed on the grey craggy shape
distantly barring the further way —
very small from here, but in its nature
mountainous, commanding.

Away he went, looping and winding
to and fro between path and stream,
and always nearing the Rock,
that slowly, slowly grew, suddenly
becoming just that — a huge rock,
challenge, playground, something to use.

He scrabbled up its fissures and ledges,
whooped, whistled, ran along its crest,
paused once in a while to see
the wilderness that lay beyond,
slithered down, gathered breath
for the slower trudge down-valley.

At the gate, he looked back
at the grey shape that stretched,
tiny in the distance, across the valley.
'Now it's big again', he said, and smiled.

Scars

There are long scars
on the hill's pelt. Despite
centuries of grassing-over,
these gapped wounds, their verges
swollen, still bring a thought
of inflammation, soreness, pain.

Not far away, tall foundations
rear from a mighty ditch.
Only a remnant remains of stone
long ago torn out, perhaps,
scarring the hill, from those
enigmatic cuts into the flesh
of its passive bulk.

Perhaps. Year after year
scholars and devotees
of these high solitudes have wondered,
argued. Year after year
lenses have focussed on grassy trench,
swollen lip. Year after year,
eager debate has dwindled
along windy reaches of upland air.

Probably quarries? Nothing certain.
No proof possible. The castle ruins give out
with unambiguous strength
their echo of old defiance.
                      It is the unexplained
wounding that haunts, refusing to yield
the benison of understanding.

.

Undefined

Probably this photograph
is of the woman, though
she is so small, so far,
she could be incidental.

From the road above
a grassy slope, she seems
to be looking down at him.
His lens is turned towards her,
but doesn't zoom in
to lessen the distance between them.

That may be the subject —
distance: the small figure
below sombre crags
above the long steep drop
to the river.
           No certainty
of any interchange;
maybe a look? Maybe.
Only the lens,
making its moment's précis,
has definition.
The hinted story has none.

Cadences

Is any landscape
inexhaustible? Surely
there comes a time
when each stone repeats
its brother's song, in which
the cadences are dulled?

Yet there's no limit
to probings, responsive
frissons, of the endlessly
wondering mind,
endlessly craving heart.
They listen to the lasting
music of their own
home hill, home stream,
with the once-and-always
assent of love.

Dogs' Voices

Delivering a message, we climbed
to discover the house, remote and high.
No-one was at home that afternoon.
Blinds drawn against May sun. Deep quiet.
We knocked at front door, side door, tried
locked gate to a back alleyway.

That woke the only sound we'd heard—
somewhere out of sight, a dog
bayed, then another, sounding huge, lordly,
suspicious; utterance hollow
like the feeling of emptiness
in the house, like echoing rooms from which
humanity was withdrawn.
                              Yet someone
must be caring for those great beasts. Some link
was alive. Someone would come home.

We turned from the house, looked down
over miles-wide expanse of field, hedge, copse,
glint of river, rooftops, hint of road—
on the horizon, hills with sunny mist
confusing scale, adding mystery. All still,
with a quiet that held and muted
a hundred sounds of life.

Abandoning our errand, we took the track
down. Faintly, as we picked our way,
came again that hollow note of warning
from the great dogs, giving silence a voice, waiting
for governance and meaning to return,
for permitted hands to gentle brindled pelts,
as sun slid into dusk.

Wrong Turn

I should not have been there,
shall not be there again,
shall not forget.
                   The lane
meandered through a thin wood,
went on too long, brought conviction
only of trespass.
                   Suddenly
the trees sat back, lane
became drive, pillared bridge
led to gravelled forecourt.
Long, low, redly creepered
in September sun,
the house glowed

No sound except a river's
understated calm-weather song.
From the bridge, deep shadow.
A mill down there, huge wheel
motionless, seeming not disused
but resting from use,
workaday, but in that dimness
not without mystery. I realised
it was the Wye that flowed
as millstream here, queen
playing handmaid.

                   Looking back
at the house before leaving,
unexpectedly I felt kinship
between its life and mine, both
being contradictory, unclear.
It lived on two levels, plunged
from sun to shade; was hard in stone,
in water shifting, mutable.
It had a kind of certainty, yet endured
tremors of hauntedness.

                    This place
had been intruded on, and yet had taken
me, chance-come questioner,
into its unknown story; destined
to stay in mine, had made an entry,
unwilled, uninvited, welcome.

Enigma

I've never been sure that, when the brain
drops into death, it takes with it
all that jumble of half-remembered
sights and sounds, half-shaped ideas, hauntings,
atmospheres, premonitions—the hinterland
of a departing life.
                    More likely, I've thought,
that gallimaufry escapes dark sleep, floats free,
its diverse entities gone sliding—can it be
randomly?—through chinks and windings
into a living brain, bringing bafflement, or even
once in a while unlooked-for hope of meaning.

Whence does that quirk of roadway come
I've visualised so often, twisting up
past a pale field of unfamiliar corn
and damply mirroring a darkening sky?
This picture has no feeling of memory, seems
to have no part in any life of mine.

Yet it has forced an enigmatic,
determined way into this brain that works
and works at it, finding no answers,
only a sense of what may be mine
by adoption—a possible meaning
endlessly to be sought, for a richness
hidden within it, wanted, apprehended,
not yet understood.

Triptych

with thanks to photographs in Phil Cope's Borderlands

1. Portrait of a Devotee

The well-seeker has found her pool,
unobtrusive but sacred.
She stands in contemplation,
head bowed towards the brownish,
gently stirring water, hands lightly clasped,
not so much in prayer as modestly
suggesting that state.

It isn't easy here to be sure
of the feeder-stream's course—towards
the well it mazily wambles,
now visible, now half-hidden in clumps
of wetland foliage. From the pool
there starts a rocky tumble down
to join a flow more definite
than anything in this upland place.

Behind the tussock where the woman stands,
seen past her shoulder,
both trunks of a split tree are presences,
each lifting out to either side
branches upturning like a pair of wings.

2. Oswald's Well

A sweep of wild common, green
broken by long straw-like grass,
tinged with red by the well
of a martyred king—as though
there is never quite an end
to Penda's butchery.

A hole like a black grave; water
unseen. Inadequate fencing
makes no attempt at symmetry.
Far off, one stark house stares.

What in the picture makes
the most insistent claim
on our eyes? Is it
the solitary house, that should spell
humankind, normality, yet offers nothing
of reassurance?
     Or the profound hole
of the well, cancelling sight
in black deeps?
     Or is it the line
of hedgerow trees, echoing
the hurry of driven clouds
over a livid sky? Some trees are too short
to feel the strenuous wind's assault,
yet in their sombre bushiness
seem not at rest.
     What of the taller ones?
Go, go, go! shouts the wind,
and they strain to obey, lurching
forward, away, as if hating their own
rootedness, that allows no escape.

Escape? Perhaps there is none here
for anything—distant staring house;
sky, huge, disturbed; well-water
lurking in blackness; boundary-trees
vainly struggling away from fear;
land uneasy, tainted with blood
unredemptive, never wholly
soaking away.

3. The Yew

Young when the Romans left? The pictured yew
seems older than that—not constrained
at all by time.

                    Its grip on the hill
is passionate. Its massive bulk
suggests excess. The trunk, with its harsh bark,
is composite—knots, ridges, bulges, looking tortured,
are flung together and meld.
Branches are of fearful proportion,
obscure patterns of growth.

                    Some, at the brink
of the hill, have a rushing movement, cling
close to the slope, as though caressing it,
follow it down to an unseen well.

The tree is garlanded, swollen mossy limbs
flaunting red ribbons and white, a dangling heart,
a hotchpotch of offerings from givers
who come to weep, thank, celebrate, implore;

who have some sense, perhaps, of the great yew's
terrible love of transient earth, of its fierce craving
to stay for ever clutching the hill,
for ever sweeping down to hidden waters;
as if it longs, and knows the longing vain,
for a gnarled, rooted, earthbound eternity.

Now

Waking from a muddle of dreams
to a fogbound search
for meaning, one may find
forming, beyond the murk
of an unpropitious day, a blur of sun.

Sensations proclaim themselves—
drizzle whisking by
as a wind gets up: drift
of small leaves;
clunk, settling of poles
on a timber-lorry passing;
click and whoosh of an opening door.

There's a jangle of notes, off-key,
unbeautiful but live; tap of a pencil
dropped on wood; rattle of rings
as a window is bared,
and sun's rays reach at last
through misted panes to light
the undeniable now.

Ambivalence

'I believe
she's twenty,' I say,
and mean 'I'm not sure'.
'I believe
God made the world,' she says,
and means he did,
no scrap of doubt.

I love the ambivalence
of words, of this,
that surely should hold
certainty. I love the way
'I don't quite know' is one
with 'I know for sure'.

Is this where to find
truth? In the box
with Schroedinger's cat,
poisoned now, silent, stiff,
and furrily stretching now,
miaowing?

Truth

Half-asleep, I saw
a hilly street, bookshop, clock-tower,
a bird or two cutting into cloud,
and you were there, where you never were.

I thought of age, the friends who die,
the ones who leave, the ones
just ill-drawn sketches in the mind.

How jumbled is truth! Now
anyone can be anywhere, actuality
being so transmuted.
                        You might as well
climb that hill. Nothing will be served
by stringent editing. Draw breath
at the clock-tower, launch your mind
to fly with the birds I too
may never have seen.

Gulls' Voices

A steep road curves down—to the sea?
If it is there, it's hidden
by a high wall, but all the time
I hear crying of gulls.
                      On the right,
small houses, some stone-grey,
some whitewashed.
                      At the corner
of a side-lane, an empty shop,
window's ornate frame
picked out in gold,
green door shut.

This is what I came for—
our meeting-place?
I am too late.

My disappointment is loud
in the gulls' cries, dulls
trim cottages, fades hope
of onwardness for the road.

This is a dead end, full-stopped
by the hidden sea.

Was there ever a life
in which the true story
went otherwise?

What I see, hear, is surely
a fantasy of regret.

Is there a rebel dream
where the door opens?
What might I hear then
in the voices of gulls?

White Bird Flying

From behind and above me
suddenly it flew,
straight and purposeful,
past and on, vanishing
into shadow, that white bird.

I still don't know
if this is memory, dream,
visualisation, just
that some sort of reality
flashed in and by and was gone.

Should I identify
symbols? Or get lost
in tangle of the past,
looking for a link,
forcing reluctant meaning?

Why? My mind gave me
a tiny sudden happening,
an enigma made of light and speed,
with its own sealed significance,
not to analyse, only to keep.

The Lizard

It pressed against my windowpane,
out there late in the damp and cold,
the impossible lizard. A hand-length,
more perhaps, it was nothing like
the tiny real creatures that used to run
on our dusty lanes in the hot summers.

This one could never be a true part
of cold unwelcoming dusk.
It could not be here. It must
be a visual trick, a fantasy
made by shifting leaves in an edgy wind
that was bringing the autumn dark.

The pads of its little feet,
its soft dank-looking toes, clung.
Its pale long belly shone, almost,
caught by the gleam of a light
from across the room. Its throat pulsed
faintly. As if that minuscule movement
were too much, the illusion
broke into nothingness.

Now the only motion was the sway
of leaves again, out there.
Nothing was left but the possible,
believable; nothing to feel but a sense
of something withdrawn before fully seen,
a small deprivation.

Pheasants

The cock-pheasant rears and dips his head,
regal in red and purple-green,
but his majesty is compromised. Something
he spied under dead leaves is too alluring.
He scratches them up, busily,
domestically, poultry-wise;
plunges his beak in the dank mass
unsuccessfully, reverts to frantic
inappropriate scratching.

His three hens keep their distance.
Beige wraiths, they weave wispily
between bare hedge-stems. In a while
one separates herself, materialises
as a small, neat, unostentatious creature
(with nothing of splendour yet something
of dignity), and hesitantly moves
across the grass to stand staring
at her master, who shows no slightest
awareness of her.

         A long minute or two
and she turns away. Soon she rejoins
the others in their insubstantial,
self-sufficient windings.
                Easy to think
that in her fashion she has made
a comment, unheeded, valid,
and will waste no more time.

Escapes

Dim light.
On the mat by the stove
a small raised blob,
colour uncertain; in half-dark
shape imprecise. Did it stir?
Could it have legs, folded—
spider-legs? Could it be
sitting in a scrunch,
ready to expand, scuttle?
Fighting familiar shudders
I braced myself to get it out
in a glass, securely capped,
causing it no harm.

Then, definitely, movement.
Not a scuttle, not a leggy dart—
unmistakably, a hop!

Reaching the lamp's circle
it sat, a recognisable,
beautiful, very small frog.
Caught, squirming protestingly
in my warm hand, it was lifted
out of the house, released
into cool air, damp leaves, night,

leaving a satisfying sense
of escapes—the frog's
from starving shrivelling death
in the alien aridity of my house,
mine from a confrontation, from guilt
at feeling for that possible spider,
a creature harmless, intricate,
life-involved, vulnerable, nothing
but a qualm of phobic distaste.

Toad in May

Weeks of drought; now
this unreal day of sultry sun
and thunder building.

Battery almost dead,
the radio, tilted on clumps
of yellowed grass, has rasped
to a harsh whisper.
                      Reaching
to switch it off, the girl
sees, half-hidden by wilting leaves,
a bulging toad, that seems
uncensoriously listening.

In case this is no illusion,
in case a small creature,
warty, pulsing, rapt,
has any sort of pleasure
in such a sound, on this tedious
unpropitious day,

she leaves her radio on and goes,
allowing the scrapiness to grate,
in its own time, into silence,
and the toad to make what it will
of a lack, an ending.

Dice Game on Dinas

The climbing field-path lost itself
in a plashy place, rich in spring
with a fat wiggling of tadpoles.
Above that rose another track
up a heathery hillside, often fired,
blacker then than the coal-valley beyond.

                    Sometimes by the track
in a small quarry, would sit a ring of workless men,
whippets spare and strung at their sides—
all still except the flicker of nerves
through the dogs' pelts, and the quick outthrust hand
of one man, throwing the dice.
They had no words, no eyes for a passer-by;
only sometimes a whippet would turn
its delicate medieval head to stare.

High above plain and sea, the men
sat like carved kings, until
a sharpened breeze, and the nearing of night
brought the time to trudge their homeward track—
no more from an ended shift, yet chill
with the ghost of that weariness. Now and then
one or other would turn with a word,
including in fellowship his quiet dog at heel.

Enjoy

'Enjoy!' said a massive stranger,
making way for me to pass
up the black iron spiral stair
towards the Search Room, where I hoped
for bits of certainty to piece together
forgotten lives. 'Enjoy!' He spread
to shoulder-height the great black
bat-wings of his cape, and smiled.

I smiled too, at the brief, extraordinary
meeting, the moment of shared savouring
heightened by the oddness
of that huge black-winged figure
and his benevolent word,
a gift I have kept for years.

The Ash-Tree

The tallest tree by far
in the line beyond the field,
                    always the ash
has such a short summer:
                    always, though,
there seems a queenliness
In its reluctance to assume
the softness of leaf.

                    'An untidy crown'
says the tree-book. I don't think that,
liking the way its topmost spread
of bare twigs rakes the cloud.

This year the whole tree
has been bare so long I have feared
it dead of the ash-plague, imagined
a withering finality, a 'never'
in the dark of its boughs, lifted starkly up
past the lively clustering greens
of other trees.

                    But yesterday,
still more today, sharp silhouettes
are blurred a little, have a gleam
of tender colour, tiny beginnings
of summer grace, that wake
a disproportionate response—relief,
happiness even.

                Not a dream,
not a window on paradise, not
an omen of joy—this is nothing
but a tree that might have died
lifting late leaves against a summer sky.

Sleepers

They have gone to sleep now,
the boy neatly curled,
the small girl suddenly falling
into sprawled stillness.
For this evening, a sitter
is guardian of the sleepers
on an island in the moors:
and of three tidlings bleating from the barn,
unconcerned cats, tense young sheepdog
lying on the yard, facing the track,
alert for the homeward car.

The lambs give up calling.
In the hall a guinea-pig grumblingly
chitters from its covered hutch,
then accepts sleep. Now
there is only the wind
in the thin horseshoe of trees
sheltering a half-made garden.
All round, rushy moorland
flows into night.

          Late,
it's the dog who catches the car's
tiny distant burr. Barking
sets the lambs crying again,
but the children sleep on.
Their mother keeps her promise,
whispering into deaf ears, 'I'm home.'

Country Church at Night

Not so much silence
as voices, hushed.
Not so much voices
as emptied sound.
Not so much sound
as pulsing in dark.
Not so much pulsing
as stillness, alive.
Not so much dark
as starlight, waiting.

Landscape in Spring

One more upward twist of the road
and over the crest the view flicks open
like the spread of a fan.
The rippling-away of hills,
cleft of a valley, solitary house
small and white on a distant slope,
the way a gentle landscape
can seem vast in benign sunshine
of spring—this is for the eye's joy.

But plunging down into all that
is more for the heart, never free
of that shadow of knowledge
that spring passes: more like longing,
more like love.

Leaving for Home

1.

> *...my country is far away*
> *time to begin the journey home*
>   Anne Beresford, 'The Comforter'

Why should it be sad
to think of going home?

Is it because now
this is what I know,
when once it was surely
strangeness, exile?

Is it because you are here,
and I can't see you
by that hearth
I just remember?

Is it because I no longer know
who might come down
that once-known path
as here you do,
bringing the light?

2.
> *...if thou wilt, remember...*
> Christina Rossetti, 'When I am dead')

ash on the wind
walk away
say only, This
is like her touch
brushing by
asking nothing

ash on the stream
walk away
say only, This
is like her love
a flowing song
wordless

Reading Traherne

'We are Flames and Lights and Thrones
to each other,' said Traherne,
seeing in all of them the Sun
and ministering Angels.
                    He lived
in a world of astonishment.
Still, by his words, slaves to the ordinary
are lifted from their chains.
Loss, timidity, doubt shrivel
in hot light of a vision whose terror
has made an alchemical change
into love.

Moor at Dusk

At dusk, from a higher hill,
I can see, blurred in failing light,
the moor's rise and fall towards
a hardly discernible horizon.
Bleak beauty has gained from night's approach
sombre intensity.

A narrow road streaks down and away
into distance, bearing one car that soon
becomes a dwindling light.

There seems nothing here to be perceived
with the eye only. I recognise
something dark as the land,
uncompromising, beyond reason,
like the triumph or breaking of the heart.

Stones on the Moor

Those who set the great stones here,
who with such killing labour brought them
miles over upland moors in rainy wind
or unrelenting sun, mustered all their
strength and nascent skills to lift them
(with sweat, gasps, groans) on rough
contraptions, desperately devised—

they, authors of this venture,
driven by need we only guess at, knew
what power their broken breath invoked
as the stones reared up at last against the sky—
a silent enigmatic statement,
over millennia unchanged. Speculation
aims feebly at meaning, misses the mark.

To speak for so long, in such desolation,
a language of total mystery; to relate
as ever to peaty earth, calm or stormy sky;
to have been, to be, the same; is this
what gives the stones their strange
reassurance, serenity, the way
they absorb us into forgotten power?

Limestone

Auden, trying to imagine a faultless love,
saw a limestone landscape, heard
underground streams.

Poring over pictures
of another such landscape,
Welsh sister of his Derbyshire hills,
I wonder that I held so long
to that concept of faultlessness,
thought it spelt in land like this.

Broken structures, detritus of spoil,
mark what has been worked,
abandoned. Sink-holes crowding
in anfractuous lines
match windings of water in depths beneath.
Here and there a vast hole
has swallowed—what?—
when the bedrock sank. Now
it threatens like an open-jawed mouth.

Surely if this landscape,
disturbing in scarred beauty,
has any link with love,
that love must be flawed—
damaged, unstable, addictive,
inescapable, real.

Abundance

1. Making May

May, when Lucifer fell, they say:
when wolves are born.
May, anciently
the unlucky month
of hawthorn spells,
of chill taboo,
unchosen chastity.

Then metamorphosis,
hawthorn asserting
scent of the female,
devotees half-smothered
in sheaves of it, flung
in whirling dance
that caressed the towering pole.

Where now are those contraries?
Have they blended to make
this May of ours, flowing in dappled ease
along a road under arch after arch
of green-gold boughs?
                      Nothing here
of barren deprivation. Down each dip
of the road, round every curve, there comes
a soft echo of dancing elation.

2. The Golden Horse

Trees July-green, deep but not yet
dusty and heavy. High along the bank
across a green lane, a pony galloped
out of trees into sun, on into trees, and was gone.
I know that happened—in its way true.
I know it's over.

But that was a day of exhilaration,
full to the brim of summer.
I know I saw a gold horse flying,
flying through green air, sun, green air,
vanishing to a changeless place
in the rejoicing mind. I know that's real.
I know it will never be over.

3. Apricot Climate

Yours is the apricot climate
of fortunate gardens warm-walled
on a sunward hill. You are defined
by happiness, moulded by hope;
with you, winter seems
dark alien fantasy.

Frost cracks all summer spells.
Temper your pride, make offering
at noon to the gods of golden weather,
that they may not leave you,
that you may still walk
through glancing light
of your apricot years.

4. Cider Mill

Because it's grey and stone, and sits
coldly in dimness of a forgotten
outbuilding, the cider-mill
seems unconnected to the golden life
of harvest quaffing, to spin of mind and senses
through green tree-tunnel out
under deep-drunk blue to blaze of sun,
heat of hay. What summer wildness
could have been woken by this chill round
of unresponsive stone?
                                  And yet the mill
has the shape of eternity, circle in circle,
never beginning, never knowing an end.
Perhaps after all it offers an idea
of wholeness? Perhaps in the cold twilight
of a dusty room it silently
celebrates ecstatic fruition,
nourishes within its greyness
unforgotten gold?

The Train

After her husband died
she told me it seemed to her
he was on a train, huge,
transcontinental, slowly
gathering speed, relentlessly
receding into unknowable distance.
Was destination implied?
No return was scheduled.

Over years she became,
on the surface, much as she'd been—
many-friended, loving a laugh
(but never happy, she said to me,
never again happy).
                    Sometimes,
coming into the room, I'd see her
standing at the window, tense,
concentrating, as if once more
she'd caught sight of the train,
a hardly distinguishable dot
vanishing into desert
of immeasurable distance.

Verity

Almost he persuaded her,
almost. The utter reasonableness of his
material certainties (if such they were),
his wonder at the deftness, intricacy
of the world's workings, but calm acceptance
of lack of planning, planner's non-existence—
all this had its own reassurance.
                                  She
had no certainty. She never asked
just what he felt when violin or voice
seemed climbing into a world of otherness,
and his face momentarily showed—
or so she thought—astonished recognition.
Fleetingly she'd seen his hold
fragile as hers on shadowless verity.

Lark Ascending

How to tell the child
about skylarks?—the way,
as they climbed the sky,
the song too spiralled, not only
rising with the singer, but made
of notes with an upward curl?
How to tell her
about soft brownness, fragility
of a small bird, its nest
a treasure to find, out on the moor?

She knows 'bird'; kites have been back
for years now, over crumbling towns
(they find food enough)—but the word
means hugeness to her, swooping, rending,
something she crouches away from.

The high moor is out of bounds,
except to hunters; fields and woods
are feral, hazardous. Children
don't go outside the wall before
they can be trained to kill.
Since the virus, home means huddling
within the reassurance of streets. We patch,
we barricade; there are so few of us.

Rumour runs along nerves. Out there,
in the risky lands of our cautious forays,
some sense impending change.
We are wary, knowing whatever comes
may not be enemy, but is not friend.

She has yet to know this, as she grows:
Yet surely in crannies of her mind
I can plant images to flourish
of light-winged upward springing,
unthreatening vastness, horizons
attainable and worth the journeying.

Waiting for the Tide

In clear sunlight of the dream,
seven discs, leaf-like, were floating
on a green-blue sea.
At the centre of each
stood a tiny woman,
her robe swirling,
her long hair lifting
in a shifting breeze.
Across the picture, words—
'Waiting for the tide'.

Nothing to hint
what that waiting might bring,
no message, promise, warning,
yet an insistent sense
of withheld meaning, a longing
for inclusion in this mystery,
for the tide to make itself known.

Happy Ending

How must it be for those who thought
the dark their destiny?—how must it be
when a tremendous dawn breaks, unforeseen?

They who believed that love, surprise, delight
were lost for ever; now are hardly able
to comprehend such joy and how to greet it.

This dazzling change is slow to let them dare
accept as theirs the integrity of light,
trust the validity of happiness.

And yet at last surely it seems the dark
never claimed victims, never shut them in,
but light alone is certitude and home.

Or so they dream, and dreaming, cannot doubt.

Elms

I think it was just there,
where the lane (under the houses now)
used to curve and climb,
that the old wall started,
beyond it, broken barns.
Between wall and yard were elms,
brittle-branched, dangerous in gales.
It seems always November
when my mind sees them, always
blowing up for a storm, though many times
I walked there, and must have known
gentler weather. Why return
to the November swirl and shout
of savage trees, long ago cut down,
if not for an unremembered happiness,
warm as honey-bee summer,
waiting there in the cold?

Extremes

Out of shade, the track
ran down to a shimmering house,
glare of white walls, utmost
rigour of heat. In a treeless field
a solitary pony looked stunned,
motionless except for grudged effort
of draggle-tail swish at flies.

We had inched the car under trees
and sat on the bank, torpid, plan-less.
I had known other seasons here—
spring with mild warmth gentling the land,
small clear bird-notes, quiet light;
autumn's drama and its gift
of returning vistas, hills framed by branches
when vivid leaves fall.

But today, extreme bred extreme.
I sensed through heavy stillness of heat
a deeper silence of winter; envisioned
dark daytime skies, weird uniformity
of white, with its own chill glare,
transforming field after field,
climbing and capping distant hills,
outlawing for long
the vocabulary of thaw.

Today's reality and imagining
were alike savage—maybe the truest mode
of apprehending a countryside
always beautiful, rarely benign;
where extremes stubbornly claim inalienable
rights of return.

Encroachment

The old families are passing, almost gone.
One left here, one there, the rest
thistledown blowing.

On hillside, by river, under trees,
are sale-boards, smartened houses, 'people from off'
who come, think to settle, muster each
a count of years shorter at times
than the former count of generations.

The road down-valley has the air
of narrowing, so close now press
the rustling trees, so strongly the stream
sweeps, so lush and deep
is the bordering grass.

Old patterns blur, admit
unease of the half-seen,
hardly guessed-at.
              For centuries
wilderness has suffered
man's puny incursions.
Is it now penetrating
vulnerable enclosures,
leaping fragile boundaries?
Is it now encroacher,
bringing in the unknown?

Defiance

She'd explored an empty valley—
rough grass, wind-brushed:
a scattered ruin: stumbling flow
of a grey stream: from either bank
slow rise of stony land.

In the desolation
she'd heard a baby crying.

When she spoke of it
there were indulgent smiles.
I think I believed her;
it seemed not to matter
whether she heard with ears or heart.

I knew that valley—its resilience,
its naked strength.
To this near-barrenness
life had come early, survived, spread.

I had dreamed of a time
when our world might be
a whisper away from destruction,
yet in wilderness places, life,
with a new defiant crying,
might launch again
its tiny assault on the void.

sequence), it is not just human existence that is kept alive: for here, in a gloriously celebratory penultimate stanza, Bidgood names and commemorates the railway engines that ran on the eponymous but short-lived Grwyne Fawr Light Railway that was built in the early twentieth century to enable construction of the dam for the Grwyne Fawr Reservoir, high up the valley: 'Come, Dukinfield, / unstable but dauntless, cling to the rails / on the giddy gradients. / Come, trim Anita / stay trusty on the mail-run morning and night. / Come, little Brigg, / beaten by a blizzard, try again.' Here, as elsewhere in her work, Bidgood is crucially attentive to the small stories of near-forgotten lives, which she holds again up to the light. In this sense, she is very much a remembrancer for the sort of place that she describes, in the poem 'All Manner of Thing', as one that is 'forgotten in a wrinkle / of a small country's mountains'. In the Black Mountains poems, of course, Bidgood reaches beyond the 'small country' of Wales—an issue that she engages with explicitly in the poem 'Merthyr Clydawg', as she considers a region over the border that is nonetheless one of 'shifting boundaries' with 'Welshness in the soil's depth'. But that commitment to bringing into sight that which might be too easily forgotten—places, buildings, the lives of individuals and communities, things past and nearly out of view—that commitment is a key quality both of Bidgood's overall poetic output and of many of the poems collected here.

Matthew Jarvis
Aberystwyth, July 2016

'Patricio 2001' is again about the responses of contemporary people—this time the focus being responses to the holy well at Patricio (Partrishow). However, what is perhaps most pertinent about 'Patricio 2001' in this context is that the poem considers people's reactions during what its speaker calls 'a time of fear and shattering' which, given the overt date reference of the title, gestures towards the September 2001 attacks on New York's Twin Towers—a connection that Bidgood herself confirms. In short, for all her engagements with the past, Bidgood never leaves the pressures of the present behind.

However, just as important as these contemporary references is the fact that Bidgood's poetic focus—past and present—so frequently brings to light ordinary lives, the small stories of humanity. 'Patricio 2001' and 'Time and the Running Child' are precisely examples of this, with the former giving space to the responses of anonymous people in a time of crisis, whilst the latter celebrates the minor (though nonetheless important) pleasures of a holidaying youngster at her friend's house. But this quality is perhaps most striking in terms of engagements with the past, in the sense that lost lives, lost voices are thus pulled back into the light and given articulation. For example, in 'Cwmioie' (from the 'Singing to Wolves' sequence)—which is a response to St Martin's church in the eponymous village of Cwm-iou (Cwmyoy) in Monmouthshire—it is entirely typical of Bidgood's work that, considering a memorial, the poet-speaker gives voice to a dead child ('one-year-old Mary', one of 'three small girls of one house [who] came home / early from play'), who 'cries "I was but young", / and claims eternal rest, being too tired / too soon'. However, the poem does not just seek to give words to the child—words that a one-year-old would not, of course, have spoken. Rather, the final lines go even further to restoring her identity in the present as Bidgood hears, in the breeze, 'a susurration of grass, not unlike / whispers or stifled laughter'. Here, in other words, the dead girls are imagined at play once again, their lives made to echo once more into the present. Likewise, in 'Merthyr Clydawg', the next poem in the same sequence, Bidgood attends to two lost lives whose memory has literally been brought back into the light, as 'Latin / on a dug-up stone remembers / 'that faithful woman the dear wife / of Guinnda'. Indeed, in the poem 'G.F.L.R.' (in the 'Guérinou' 'beautiful desolation' that the 'first anchorites had loved'. Similarly, 'Blaenllyfni Castle' is precisely an engagement with the eponymous ruins, whilst 'Tŷ'n-y-Llwyn' (from the 'Guérinou' sequence) responds to an 'ancient house' that was —at the point of the poem's composition—lying empty. Thus, although some signs of care remain in 'topiary still roughly trimmed' and 'the small lawn mowed not too long since', there are 'nettles thrusting across the steps' and the house offers only a 'dull / echo-less thud' in response to the poet-speaker's knock. Nonetheless, the poem's final stanza does not see this emptiness as life 'ended' but rather as life 'in abeyance'. As such, the poet-speaker hears 'within silence, songs; / within stillness, running feet, / corners turned, doors flung wide, / the whirl of time funnelling down again, / filling the rooms'— a poetic sense of *what could yet be* that was to be subsequently fulfilled when the house was later bought and re-inhabited. Another such house—although this time derelict—forms the subject of 'The Hermitage' (in the same sequence), with the poem's speaker discovering a building that was 'more elegant in dereliction / than we'd supposed'. But perhaps more important is the close of the piece which affirms what is, for Bidgood, the articulacy of places such as this—the capacity of buildings, in effect, to speak for themselves: 'To imagine / presences, echoes, would seem / presumption. Structures, tangible, / broken, are speech enough.'

Alongside Bidgood's focus on the past, however, it is also important to emphasise her engagements with contemporaneity, which become brightly apparent in occasional flashes. 'Treachery' is probably the most obvious example here, with its mountain-bikers riding in a 'phalanx' down the Grwyne Fechan valley—'black-clad, impassive, / hissing dizzily past'. But likewise, in 'Time and the Running Child', it is precisely the pleasure of the eponymous child in the present that is the poem's focus, with the potential challenges of the past—manifest in her visit to a grand Victorian house—laughingly accepted from the very beginning ('*More ancestors!* laughed the visiting child, / running down a staircase flanked by portraits'). Similarly, of course, 'Llanthony' is crucially bound up with children in the present and their various responses to the priory's ruins, whilst

The poems themselves suggest many of the major concerns that are identifiable in Bidgood's broader poetic output: in other words, whilst they may form a distinct geographical grouping, they are not in any way disconnected from Bidgood's overall poetic character. Perhaps the most obvious quality they share with her wider work, then, is their recurrent interest in the past. The very first of the pieces collected here, 'Olchon Valley', draws on the seventeenth-century religious life of the place ('a towering fire, / such a fire in the valley'), before turning to a present in which that 'flame' has gone out entirely, leaving the poem's speaker contemplating a different fire—a potent but unspecified force that draws 'us' into the valley's non-human 'congregation'. Similarly, 'Llanthony'—from the 'Singing to Wolves' sequence—begins with the monks of the eponymous Augustinian priory who, in the twelfth century, temporarily left their remote location for (in the poem's words) 'soft living at the daughter-house'. Perhaps more striking still is 'Garlanding the Urn', in which the past stands as a concretely physical presence in day-to-day life, as the church-turned-house to which the poem responds now incorporates a memorial on its kitchen wall as well as the bones of the dead below the floor. Thus, pertinently, the poem's final stanza sees the particular situation of the house as 'an acceptant union / of what was with what is'—in other words, an amicable co-existence of past and present. Or as Bidgood has put it, talking about the incident which inspired the poem, she asked the owners of the house 'about the Parrys'—a historic family associated with the church—'and was told there were one or two in the kitchen!'

Another familiar characteristic of the poems here is that Bidgood's interest in the past (and the continuation of the past into the present) is often manifest through her concern with buildings –'Garlanding the Urn' being an example of precisely that. However, it is worth noting that the buildings which draw her attention are quite frequently empty or derelict, or are actually ruins, such as the case with 'Llanthony' where, in the poem's present, all but one of the children play energetically amongst the 'tidied ruins' of the priory. The exception is 'One tiny girl' who kneels quietly and alone 'in the shade of the chapter-house wall' and who thus, to the poem's speaker, seems to connect with the 'remote, solitary, / trackless', the relatively early on in her writing life, into the outer, most westerly reaches of the Black Mountains region—the former suggesting the experience of a visit (observing 'tree-stumps', 'walls held up by trees'), the latter responding rather more to Llyn Syfaddan as a place within Welsh mythology, in the sense that the poem is a rendering of the tale told by Giraldus Cambrensis about the lake's birds singing in recognition of a true prince of Wales.

However, the momentum of Bidgood's engagement with the Black Mountains region only started to build from the 1990s onwards. 1996's *The Fluent Moment* added four poems to the group—'Olchon Valley', 'Sweetness (Trefeca Fawr)', 'Rights of Way', and the collection's title poem – and crucially represented a widening geographical engagement with the area. As such, these pieces took in, respectively, the Olchon valley (lying to the immediate east of the long Hatterall Ridge, along the top of which runs the Wales-England border), Trefeca Fawr (close to the westerly Afon Llynfi, some three-and-a-half miles north of its exit from Llyn Syfaddan), the northerly region near Hay-on-Wye, and Michaelchurch Escley (which lies two rivers further east of the Olchon, on the Escley Brook). *Singing to Wolves* (2000) added eight more poems, including the five-piece title sequence—a set of poems that, Bidgood has explained, 'arose from a day church-crawling with three friends' in the Honddu valley, Michaelchurch Escley, and Clodock. The large *New & Selected Poems* (2004), which contained thirty-eight pieces in its section of new material, added another seven poems to the group, in the form of the 'Guérinou' sequence. And whilst 2009's *Time Being* only added the solitary 'Road to the Lake' (one of the Llyn Syfaddan cluster), 2012's *Above the Forests* saw a further nine engagements with Bidgood's Black Mountains—these scattered variously around the area, from the upper reaches of the Grwyne Fechan valley ('Bridges'), down to the south beyond Abergavenny ('Rainbow'), and out to the west where the grand Treberfydd House stands close by Llyn Syfaddan ('Time and the Running Child'). In short, Bidgood's poetic engagements with the Black Mountains area have gathered both pace and geographical scope over the past couple of decades, and are a particular feature of her most recent work.

*

easterly limits are represented by Michaelchurch Escley, Clodock in Herefordshire ('Merthyr Clydawg'), and Monmouthshire's White Castle ('White Castle')—the landmark to which the latter poem responds standing some three miles east of the outlying peak of Ysgyryd Fawr ('isolated Skirrid, the Holy Mountain', in Williams's words). However, in the south, the poems push as far as Abergavenny ('Angel and Invisible Tree') and even beyond, as 'Rainbow' concerns itself with St Mary's church in Monmouthshire's Llanfair Cilgedin—which lies a little beyond the southern limit of Williams's Black Mountains map itself.

Within these broad bounds, then, there are particular clusters of geographical interest that can be identified in the overall body of Bidgood's Black Mountains work. Those around Llyn Syfaddan I have already noted. But the Honddu valley, right at the heart of the area, also inspires a number of pieces: three poems titled for Capel-y-ffin, as well as 'Llanthony' and 'Cwmioie'. Likewise geographically central to the region as a whole is the seven-poem 'Guérinou' sequence which responds to places in the Grwyne Fawr and Grwyne Fechan valleys. Indeed, within the Grwyne Fawr valley is the tiny village of Patricio (Partrishow), which is itself the focus for four of the poems collected here (two in the 'Guérinou' sequence, plus 'Angel with Wolf and Saint' and *Tout Passe*). In other words, whilst the poems as a whole are distributed widely across the broad Black Mountains area, there are a number of locales that seem to hold a particular attraction for Bidgood's writerly eye.

As well as assessing the poems' geographical reach, it is also worth assessing their reach in relation to Bidgood's poetic career. The first point to make in this respect is that the work involved here does not extend right back to the beginning of Bidgood's poetic life—by which I mean the latter part of the 1960s, following her inaugural poetic publication (of the poem 'Tree-felling') in the June 1967 edition of *Country Quest*. As such, there is nothing here from her debut collection *The Given Time*, which was published in 1972, the year she turned fifty. However, 'Blaenllyfni Castle' (from 1975's *Not Without Homage*) and 'Safaddan' (from 1978's *The Print of Miracle*) brought her,

Afterword

Ruth Bidgood is known primarily as a poet of the remote Abergwesyn area of north Breconshire—of its ruins and stories, of its pasts that echo still into the 'given time' of the present. But as her long life of poetry writing has gone on, another specific geographical focus has become apparent— one that is rooted in the Black Mountains region of south-east Wales and across the border into England. As Bidgood herself makes clear in her Foreword to the current volume, this is not an area that she knows well; rather, she is only a visitor to it. However, as she has put it to me, it contains places that she finds 'powerfully magnetic'.

Bidgood's poetic Black Mountains echo the capacious region covered by the map in the endpapers of Raymond Williams's *People of the Black Mountains*: for Williams, this is a region that extends as far as the Golden Valley in the east and Llangorse Lake (Llyn Syfaddan) in the west, down to Abergavenny in the south, and up to the River Wye in the north, as that long river loops beyond Clifford and travels onwards past Bredwardine. The geographical reach of the poems collected here likewise covers a wide region—one that does not just take in the Black Mountains themselves (the central area that Williams refers to as 'the hand of the Black Mountains', describing the main high ridges as extending southwards like fingers), but that also includes areas in their shadow and just beyond their flanks. Admittedly, the poems only once approach the more northerly limits of Williams's map, in the piece 'Rights of Way', which emerges from the vicinity of Llanigon, a little south of Hay-on-Wye; otherwise, Bidgood's northern reach here is represented by Herefordshire's Michaelchurch Escley in the east ('The Fluent Moment', 'Michaelchurch Escley: Christ of the Trades') and Breconshire's Llanelieu in the west ('All Manner of Thing'). However, there are a clutch of poems right at the westernmost limits of Williams's map, responding to Llyn Syfaddan itself and to locations in the surrounding area ('Safaddan', 'Blaenllyfni Castle', 'Road to the Lake', 'Garlanding the Urn', 'Time and the Running Child'). In the east, Bidgood's poetic attention is less far-reaching than Williams's map: the poems'

Tout Passe

Patricio, August 2011

Sheltering in the porch
on a grey August morning with wind
bitter as unfriendly autumn, I feel
more hope than on many a soft day
of summer illusion, more trust
than is often mine—
    born, perhaps
of the nature of this place, its air
of promises kept for centuries,
promises to be kept always,
even if the church fell piecemeal,
the great chancel-screen
rotted and crumbled,
the prized altars of stone were left
with no roof to protect them,
buffeted by gales, draped
in altar-cloths of snow.

A day may come
with little to be seen but hill,
trees, grass, random stone,
as when the story began.

Promises, hope. Yet
the centuries rolling,
the small things of my life,
its laughter, its loves, passing
on the surge of a chill wind.

Tout passe, tout casse, tout lasse.
No. Not everything. Not here.

Sweetness

Trefeca Fawr

Overhead, plaster is joyous
with ferment of fruit, opulence of harvest.
This was his farm, the Preacher.
Dizzy with the Word, he could still.
contain the crowd's excess.
What need of earth's honey?
A man threw away his harp,
a girl gave up dancing. Sweetness,
we have had great sweetness, they gloried.

But on his farmhouse ceilings
is the land's praise and challenge.
No end here to leaves' dance;
they whirl in still white while the house lasts.
Silence holds endless harvest music.
Up there in swag, row cluster, flaunt
in profusion sweet, sweet apples
for the longing mouth.

At Capel-y-Ffîn

suggested by a painting by Edgar Holloway

The gate slants one way, church another.
Sky's black, churchyard
apocalyptically shining.
Slab tombs tip-tilt; at any moment
the risen dead may break into dance
under the yews, under the lift,
spread, beat of seraphim's wings.

This is the moment after which
nothing can be the same;
when love rips through a life,
when a world bursts forth, when chaos
begins its improbable rule.

Bells fell silent, music faded
into leaf-stir, long faint water-talk
from a distant river-bend.
Wisps of smoke from the last snuffed candles
curled away. The dark grew strong,
at noon no less than dead of night. Who now
stabs and slashes with a sword of prayer?

And yet through dusty days, on inner walls
children play, winged winds of heaven dance,
hills keep their certainties, the rainbow triumphs;
and still, for this, sometimes the people come.

Rainbow

Llanfair Cilgedin

The church is disused, not derelict;
corners of notices in the porch
curl as the print fades. Locked inside
are wall-paintings—the key-holder's away.
On tiptoe outside a window one can catch
pictured curves of rainbow and hill.

This is a place of quiet, but not of peace.
Something here disturbs with a sad
ambivalence. Rough-mown, the churchyard
has islands of wilderness, where tombstones
rise out of tangle, their names
festooned, prickled, obscured.

But over there, rigidly railed in,
a dozen graves or more, with no
visible names, enigmatically
break the pattern, seeming to attempt
order, definiteness, in this acre of doubt,
yet keep their secrets.

The railings are tall; their blotched
rusting spikes, blade-shaped,
menace the sky, reach towards
a snarl of trees, one dead, the weird
contortions of its silvery branches
held up or strangled by battening holly.

Can anything unhallow
what was once consecrated? It seems
a savagery, never perhaps
wholly suppressed, has broken through.

All Manner of Thing

Llanelieu

There was no-one to be seen.
The long lane led to silent houses,
an ancient garden-wall straggled over
by greenery, red-lit by apples—all still,
all plunged into midday depth,
fullness, of sun.
         Stone steps into shade
felt like movement waking, as they climbed
to the churchyard's wide sunny circle
bordered by shadow, aged graves aslant
as if tipping into sleep—and at last
soft sound—swish and clink of an unseen river
in trees below sanctuary at the silent church.

This place, forgotten in a wrinkle
of a small country's mountains, felt
as though it could hold encircled the life,
through millennia after millennia, of a world.
Tectonic plates had shiggled and slid,
continents parted and joined, ice ages come and gone.
A long-dying sun burning on towards doom
seemed here in September to cherish
and be cherished.
Like the whisk of warm grass on skin
a hardly-formed thought brushed by—
might everything so embraced
indeed, ultimately, be well?

Rights of Way

Llanigon

He guardedly agrees
that the day is fine.
He wonders where I come from,
but will not ask. He thinks
I have left gates open,
and will check. Finding them shut
will not modify his mistrust.

Few make their way up here
to cross his yard between
old house and older barns; one
is too many. He feels as pain.
this violation of land, his land,
by ancient custom and prescriptive right.

Diffidently, in cherishing sun,
I cross to the far gate.
Crouched by an ailing tractor
sidelong he watches.
We are straitly buckled,
into antagonistic roles,
but I wave. Slowly
he raises a hand, turns away.

Time and the Running Child

Treberfydd

More ancestors! laughed the visiting child,
running down a staircase flanked by portraits.
She thought the gothic grandeur of her friend's home
entertaining. The cramped ladder-like steps to servants' rooms
of another century tempted her to explore; perhaps now,
remembering, she finds in her mind's lumber-room
unalarming ghosts, long-skirted girls in a perilous rush,
squeezing down to answer a distant demanding bell.

Child's laughter, clatter of running feet on polished wood,
muted in carpeted hall—then through the porch and out.
The gargoyled house behind her was strange enough,
full enough of unpredictable treasures, to keep her
on happy tenterhooks. This was her first sense
of the heady past, now spelt out, now hinted, the way it mixed
with beginnings, with that moment as she ran out,
weeks of holiday stretching ahead, and over horizon hills
blue sky, unfathomable, endless.

Garlanding the Urn

Llandefaelog Tre'r Graig

This lady in bas-relief
seems to be cuddling an urn
almost as tall as herself.
Her rounded arms emerge
from draperies enveloping
but nearly transparent
to enfold the unresponsive
object of her solicitude.
On closer inspection, one sees
she is setting around it
a garland of flowers; her expression
gives nothing away.

She is an unexpected sight
on a kitchen wall, surmounting
not carved eulogy, genealogical
trumpeting, but a row
of little flasks and jars; and close
neighbour to saucepan-shelf,
cooker and fridge. She's not alone—
random tablets proclaim
that somewhere underneath us lie
remains of worthies of the parish
whose church became this house.

An unlikely marriage, but not perhaps
unhappy, an acceptant union
of what was with what is—something
of the macabre, a touch of humour,
a continuing celebration (in the main
unconscious) of those far-off Parrys
and Morrises whose bones
are crumbling peacefully to dust
beneath our feet; and on the wall
an urn forever garlanded.

Capel-y-Ffîn Story

Faces crowded over the boy,
amazed, ecstatic, pleading.
He was frightened by the extreme
emotion, by his new unsought power.

Running down the slope into full sun
he had fallen, lain staring up
into dizzy white of hawthorn,
blue sky a hood above the valley.
Overpowered, his sight
struggled with too great light
that made a visionary strangeness.

It was a valley of stories. They spilled
from the cool-arched monastery
in a tide of visitations and miracles.
Each family hoped for its own marvel.
When he came home dazed, sunstruck,
inarticulate, the prompting questions
began. It grew easier to answer
once he had started. Yes, he said,
yes, it was the Lady, white like fire,
hooded in blue.

When at last he escaped in the cool
to the hillside, he was confused, crying,
heavy with muddled guilt. But soon,
far from the morning's heat,
free from those urgent voices, he felt
in the living air a power
that needed no defining,
posed no questions, only
absolved, mothered, consoled.

Treachery

It feels nearer the sun up here.
The stony track struggled up
through dark of trees towards
a growing disc of light, which swelled, broke
into majestic brightness.
Now the path levels, the valley opens.

Across the river one farm spreads yard and barns
in shadow against light. Above it rises
bare mountain, a final wall that flanks
the upper valley, curves round its distant head,
in a strange visual accord
with the valley-floor's sharp green
of re-seeded garths, proclaiming
work, settlement, fertility.

Alongside a fence that dwindles
towards the far-off valley-head, unseen
high passes, into barren distance
runs a green road. On it, down
from hidden solitudes, a dark dot
gleams and grows, zooms into a phalanx
of mountain-bikers, black-clad, impassive,
hissing dizzily past. Unmoved,
a fat ewe suckles her twins
under a track-side thorn.

In this domain of sun,
so all-encompassing, so royal,
only the traitor mind creates
in the shiver of sun on skin
shudder of ice-wind, subverts
with a sly imagining of snow.

Road to the Lake

'Don't miss the road to the lake,' he said,
'the cow-parsley's out'—straight away
I could see it, a small winding road
and white luxuriance
tossing in sunny wind
or stilled in a lull:
always the hope
of shining water ahead.

I didn't go. Rain came
and for days poured.
The glittering lake
slid away into dark.
       Now again
I'm making plans, searching maps
for the little road, though this time,
if I find it, there'll no longer be
those white drifts of blossom;
their time is over.
       Another year, perhaps,
another journey, and cow-parsley out
on the road to the lake.

White Castle

Unexpectedly
there is peace here,
penetrating, irrefutable.
Drum-towers and curtain wall
cherish a stillness.

The moat is full of irises.
Calm ripples out
over wide lands
to the horizon.

Arrow-slit archers here
were the best in the March,
but the garrison's children
have won, making a game of it.
It's their faraway laughter
the air holds.

Grass now, shadows on grass,
Stone, wind over stone.
Water, sliding of dark
under water. Silence,
voices inside silence,
Hear me, hear me...
gone.

Not worth the work, he would think, and be right.
Who now would need to cross the stream
to tides of grass and a derelict house?
No romantic whim had made him accept
his bridge-builder's role upstream, but an instinct
for what had not yet run its course, for the dumb
life of the useable unliving thing.
Past the pillars of the dead bridge
goes the pebbly chatter of the stream
with hardly a change of note.

Bridges

'That bridge,' he said,
the one you crossed going up the valley—
I built that, rebuilt anyway,
fifteen years ago. There was only
a strip left, not rnuch more
than a tightrope. So I got stones together
(lying around or fallen from bits of wall)
and I built it up. I did the arch
like it had been (yes, it's safe,
guaranteed!) and a parapet each side.
Everyone who comes here (not knowing)
thinks it's the old one. I'm glad of that.
To me it's like I helped the old bridge
not to finish, like it was meant to go on.'

I had stood on the bank, looking up
at his bridge, and seen ancient work,
dark against sun. Could he turn his skills,
I wondered now, to another bridge, downstream,
where only hints remain of bygone bulk,
sturdiness, a confident link
between house and road? There is rock
in the stream-bank; dawdling along,
I saw a grey mass as something made,
a pillar, tucking itself into earth now,
battered and reticent, inside it a tiny room
(privy or wine-store? Children's hideaway?)
On the opposite bank, even more hidden,
another pillar of the long-ago bridge.

Come, Dukinfield,
unstable but dauntless, cling to the rails
on the giddy gradients.
Come, trim Anita,
stay trusty on the mail-run morning and night.
Come, little Brigg,
beaten by a blizzard, try again.
Come, splendid Abertillery One,
Abertillery Two,
heavily bouncing on too-light rails,
flaunt your fluted chimneys,
your touches of copper and brass.

When it all ended, it was as though
green engines, red-buffered, had never amazed
children of the farms; as though
shrilling of whistles, crescendo
of effort, hiss of halting
had never changed the pattern of sound
shifting over ancient silence.
But in the upper valley's wilderness
rises the functional grandeur all this was for
the dam, remote and massive. Beyond
stretches the lake, once in a while
blue under great sunny skies, oftener
caught into grey of rain that feeds it,
soaking the mountain wastes of Guérinou.

7. G.F.L.R.

The Grwyne Fawr Light Railway, which enabled a dam to be built high up that valley, never rated a Railway Act. It was considered impossible to build and run.

Miles away along the valley
they could catch the creaky breath,
tinily growing, of the engine
battling impossible gradients
to reach the workings. A dam
in these high solitudes had seemed
fantasy. The railway never achieved
official identity, governmental
blessing. Labouring up rails
with sleepers laid on the road,
the engines huffed and groaned,
dragging incredible loads of stone
or coaches full of Grwyne navvies—
bearded Irish, a scatter of local lads.

The parenthesis in the valley's story
lasted less than twenty years.
Then the engines chugged away,
lines were ripped up, the workmen's village
dismantled. It was as though that strange life
had never come to Grwyne, as though
no children had chanted their tables,
and shoved each other in the playground;
no couples had loved in the makeshift houses;
as though late-coming conifers had always
choked the mid-valley with dark and silence.

I have no arts of conjuration,
and wouldn't want to raise this valley's ghosts.
But once, perhaps, it might be good to catch
faintly, from very far, the growing sound
of climbing engines.

As long as we can, we stay
wandering over fields that once were lawns,
peering through doorways and window-spaces,
through floorless hall to cellar,
seeing trees through undesigned
arches, guessing where stairs had climbed,
where corridors had run.
    To imagine
presences, echoes, would seem
presumption. Structures, tangible,
broken, are speech enough.
    As we drive away
mist clears; the valley's caught
into shining air.

6. The Hermitage

The valley's alive. Farms work. The small road
has no grass down the middle. Hedges
sit back obediently.
      The strangeness
may be bred of morning mist;
out of it loom steep round hills that seem
closer than the map shows.
Slinking away from them, the road
enters tall dark of trees and dips
to crisp chatter of water on stone.

Some houses create an illusion
of shunning capture, like live things
adept at camouflage.
Over the river a patch of deeper dark
becomes a fragment of wall, a window
is light between boughs.
      Without fully
knowing why, we have come miles
in search of a broken house, unsure
who built or named it, obsessed
with an idea of hiddenness,
an unreliable story.

All too appropriately, the bridge has gone;
There's only the stumble and slither now
of a wide ford.
      We reach our prey,
quiet at its hunters' mercy, a house
more elegant in dereliction
than we'd supposed, more unapproachable
than anyone could have planned.

    The day ticks on.
Pressed to frigid panes
I stare into snow. I'm snow-blind,
snow-mad. Reaching for wine
I lift the glass to my eyes,
letting hot colour change
that lonely white; then drink, pour, drink.

Flickering through branches,
faintly at evening my house-lights
signal to empty hills.
Dregs of wine spatter the floor as
I sag into black sleep.

5. Macnamara's Mistress

At the turn of the 18th-19th centuries John Macnamara of Llangoed would ride over the Black Mountains on a bridleway that became known as 'Macnamara's Road', to visit a mistress he kept at The Hermitage in the Grwyne Fechan valley.

When at dusk the first flakes
blew past my windows, I was sure
this was only a flurry, a small whiteness
on the tops, a flutter of chill
he would feel on his face as he rode
over the high pass. But soon
snow whirled too fast, too densely
for hope.
     I had heated wine —
not too heavy a hand with the spices,
he taught me, just a sweet-sharp
titillation.
     She's prettyish, his wife.
Does he take what offers?
Some say she loves only land,
that she rules like a man
their opulent acres. Some say
that's all he wants of her.
I wish I believed them.

I woke to white wastes, aching eyes, cold bed.
How long till the pass clears?
He is what defines me.
Today I'm no-one. Nothing in me
can call him. I see her
pouring his wine. Snow
obliterates me. It's as if
there's no story of me, as if nobody
will ever make one.

4. New Houses

Upstream, forestry
closes in. Allow for that.
Allow for a grey day, currents
of thundery air. Even then—
how could anyone chasing a dream
imagine that here it might be
happily captured? Unease
is spelt in the odd proportions
of a cottage, the way a house
down there by the river
suddenly looms.

Centuries back, the valley
was already feared. Surely all that
was long enough ago for hate
to have seeped away like the blood
of slaughter in those dark woods?
But slowly, slowly, inch by inch only,
the valley creeps towards peace.

Perhaps those who dream, who come here
and build, loving the place,
are carried unknowing within
that infinitesimal advance?
It seems that stone and wood have their own
knowledge; as if here houses they form
can do no other than disturb,
embodying a warning that safety
may still be a long way ahead.

3. Incident in Vengeance Wood

In the Bad Pass of Grwyne
silence: no wind in tall trees:
no stir in dark underwood.
Then, high up, one bird calls,
like a human cry.
       In a while
clinking, jinking, hoof-pad, voices.
Stones rattle on the downward path.
A song rises, and scraping of strings—
lightly stepping, Richard de Clare's
two music-boys; he following,
lofty on a black horse.
       Snapping of twigs,
swishing of leaves. All at once
shock of ambush—vengeful bellowing,
yells of hate. Death sneaks quietly
inside the din—arrow in throat, knife
slinking swiftly to heart.
       Swish of leaves,
crack of twigs, then silence. The singer's mouth
leeches to bloodied earth. No wind
in tall trees, no stir. Then, far away
high up, one bird calls,
like a last cry.

From the narrow terrace
one white butterfly dances out
across the valley.
The sun's eye stares,
and the white speck is gone.

2. Tŷ'n-y-Llwyn

Can any day as hot and silent as this
have no darkness of doubt?
The watch on my wrist tells one time;
the disc-harrow, rusty in long grass
by the blurred path, confuses the issue,
looking obstinately recoverable.

Inside yard-gates the chaff-house
has a tree growing through it. Stable walls
are strong, but inside them
my camera-flash wakes from blackness
racks and stalls in a tilting pattern of ruin.

I come closer to the ancient house,
slowly, afraid now of finding it dead—
hopeful at topiary still roughly trimmed,
the small lawn mowed not too long since;
but wary of nettles thrusting across the steps
and saddened by the only sound, the dull
echo-less thud of my unanswered knock.

Across the valley wooded hills,
silent too, climb to a glaring sky,
Here, a stony track drops sharply down
from this shelf of land towards
an unseen, unheard river.

Something just visible at a high window
might be a jug of flowers. I look back
and think it's illusion. Yet gradually
the house makes felt a reassurance
of life not ended but in abeyance—
within silence, songs;
within stillness, running feet,
corners turned, doors flung wide,
the whirl of time funnelling down again,
filling the rooms.

Guérinou

Guérinou is the ancient form of Grwyne. The conjoined rivers of Grwyne Fawr and Grwyne Fechan eventually flow as one into the Usk. Patricio, with its holy well below the church, and old house of Tŷ'n-y-Llwyn nearby, lies on the western side of the Grwyne Fawr. The ambush of the Norman lord Richard de Clare took place on the eastern side.

1. Patricio 2001

They have been bringing offerings
to the dark well, tying
rags to twigs in supplication, leaving
flowers to wilt in that chipped glass
uneasily perched on a dank ledge,
making crosses from bits of stick.

There seem so many of them, despite
the hiddenness of the place; as if
in a time of fear and shattering
these humble shapes are once more
valid—raw letters spelling out
helplessness, not yet
reshuffled into words of power.

Angel with Wolf and Saint

The angel sits by the well
communing with a wolf and a saint.
It seems like a long
recognizing of each other.

The well is half-hidden in a stone shrine.
Steps go down to dark water;
walls are slimy, colder
than their many hartstongues.
Below the hill, in trees, is a future house;
its grey walls waver with branches seen
through them. The church, too, above the well,
is as it will be; look hard
and you may see yourself, marvelling
at its ancientness and sanctity.

The angel is kin to the wolf in his wild
innocence, troubling to man. But the saint
is more than ordinary, being holy.
He is not afraid of these beings,
though each is alien. One knows
earth, cover, hunger, mating-stench
and the blood of blameless killing; the other
lives in the eternal surprise of heaven.

All three sit quiet within
the saint's prayer, a blessing
like well-water, like the cool of leaves
wavering through walls that do not exclude.

Angel and Invisible Tree

The wooden statue of Jesse in St Mary's, Abergavenny is thought to have formed the base of an entire missing tree, a design for the old reredos.

Jesse sleeps. Extruding a dynasty
has overcome him. A stump
is all that remains of the Tree.
No worm in the wood's heart
has eaten away his dream
of branchy maze, richness, sure design.
The angel at his head is awake
to see for him, so the Tree
goes on climbing, blossoming,
its boughs full of birds, people, creatures,
stories, fantastications, bunchy fruits,
extraordinary treasures. It seems to deny
nothing but death, but the angel
sees that too—the Tree cut, stripped,
planted on a black height;
and budding, sprouting again
exuberantly, looming aloft
in curly fronded complexity.
Jesse need not wake yet.
With amazement, the angel sees.

5. Michaelchurch Escley: Christ of the Trades

The mural is faded. Least defined
is the figure of Christ. He is a blaze
of pale flesh. All round him
are harder shapes, of axe-blade,
knife-blade, hammer-head, spoke, tine,
griddle-bar, saw-tooth. The blades
are turned towards him. One slanting sword
is poised by his right shoulder; its point
hovers just short of his skin. Scissors, shears
overlap the line of his arm; is he cut?
One hand, the right, presses his breast; the other
is raised, palm out—warding off, or giving
a left-handed blessing? He seems
menaced by aggressive sharpness, closing in
with intent to wound; the things of everyday
banding to shear, scrape, gash, destroy
the extraordinary. In stillness
he bears the encroachment, stands
pale on the dim wall, his body a window
letting enter invulnerable light.

4. Merthyr Clydawg

Clodock; it sounds rustic, and English.
Clydawg; the lost Welsh is back. He seems
an off-beat martyr, killed for love,
out hunting, by a jealous rival; yet,
a prince who led in battle and prayer,
his story has a spice of miracle. Oxen
(helped by a broken yoke) refused
to drag his body over the ford, insisted
that here should be his burial-place.

In the church, the gallery's music-table
might be straight from Hardy. But Latin
on a dug-up stone remembers
'that faithful woman the dear wife
of Guinnda', who centuries back
lived in this place of shifting boundaries,
strife, loss, perpetual haunting, garbled names,
Welshness in the soil's depth,
unacknowledged riches,
uncomprehended power.

3. Cwmioie

So hot! Colours are soft in haze,
long tawny grass round the tombs,
brown shoulders of boys and girls
sunning by the crooked church.
Built on tiptilted rock, it leans
every which way, buttressed,
stable after its fashion, with an air
of kindly eccentricity.

Inside, in the cool, a man
lies asleep on a pew, near
the tablet to seventeenth-century
Thomas Price, who 'takes his nap
in our common mother's lap',
his dust a compatible neighbour
for the bronzed and breathing sleeper.

'Better death than long languishing',
says Cadogan's motto. Amen to that,
on this day of heat and sleep,
amen! But after no long sickness
three small girls of one house came home
early from play. From their black memorial
one-year-old Mary cries 'I was but young',
and claims eternal rest, being too tired
too soon.
          The sleeping man wakes up. Outside,
the sunbathers have gone. A breeze mutes heat,
scampers over the graves, and starts
a susurration of grass, not unlike
whispers or stifled laughter.

2. Capel y Ffin

The stone gives nothing but a name,
initials, dates of birth and death,
and then a verse about the sweetness,
depth, of laughing. He lies, or she,
near a line of yews, whose twisted trunks—
one pot-bellied, splay-footed, others
goat-hoofed and pitted—seem
compatible with deep, wild, joyously
contorting laughter.
      Odd and true
this remembering; sad
the rattling laughter of survivors,
stones in the river's heat-struck bed,
rolling, falling about, denied the depths.

Singing to Wolves

1. Llanthony

'Why should we stay here
singing to wolves?' said Llanthony monks;
and left for soft living at the daughter-house,
finding themselves unloved by the Welsh,
and jaded with beautiful desolation—
just what the first anchorites had loved,
such wildness a treasure, not to be spoiled
by intrusive felling and tilling. All
they wanted was to contemplate heaven,
and the hills (almost as high), with herds of deer
ranging their tops.
      The tidied ruins
are a favourite summer place. On this
burning day only children have spirit
to dash under arches, burst from shade to sun,
shifting points of colour, as intense
as flowers in baskets hung in front
of the crowded restaurant.

      One tiny girl,
dark-haired, cool in a blue dress,
stays apart; alone she kneels on grass,
in the shade of the chapter-house wall,
carefully picking daisies. Perhaps she,
who knows? in her generation will be one
whose love is given to the remote, solitary,
trackless; to risk-encircled beauty;
deer on the marches of heaven; the sweet
unprofitable singing to wolves.

The Fluent Moment

Against an inner wall of the small church
leans a symbol-stone, encapsulating
all things known, at rest. Sober-faced Sun,
rayed with crisp flames, is King of a static world.

But in the porch, ivy has climbed
right through the walls, insinuating
tough stems into crevices above the arch;
and flows high up in dark luxuriance,
forcing an over-shoulder glance, a thought
of all things built to fall, falling to rise.

The future has been and has been.
There is a movement here like Escley stream
that down from slopes of Cefn arrives
and in the same fluent moment leaves.

Blaenllyfni Castle

Towers among trees among walls—
not darkness, not light,
not noise, not silence,
not life, not death—
nothing whole or definite;
fragments of a picture
shattered, or not yet composed.
Islanded in sun and grass,
an enigmatic ground,
dappled and rustling,
troubles chance-comers, shakes
complacency, breeds doubt.
A camouflage of frecked light,
shifting dark—what hides from whom?
Into the wood I bring
sun-dazzle under my eyelids, peer
at tree-stumps, fangs once towers,
branches growing from walls,
lattice-work of roots
involved with stone,
walls held up by trees,
brought down by trees—
a kind of war, a kind of love,
    an infiltration.
These are new shapes
for ancient ambiguity,
old clouding of new eyes
that can't see wood for walls,
    castle for leaves,
        for dark,
            for sunlight
now, out of the wood,
blinded by summer.

Now the third rider, tall on a tall white horse,
slowly paced down to the hushing waters,
dismounted, knelt in prayer. I shipped my oars
and was quiet as the birds. When he stood
in the growing sunlight, knowledge came to me.
I knelt in the boat. He called.
All round me, suddenly, were wings
beating the water, rustling the reeds,
and a thousand songs of homage rose.
My boat rocked on the joyful surge
of Llyfni's invisible stream, my ears
were dazed with triumphant proclamations
of sunken bells, and louder and louder
the All Hails of Safaddan's birds.
Lake and kingly rider and host of birds,
and I with them, were caught up into the sun.

Fragmented sun on sliding water:
reed-beds thick at the lake's verge:
the island low astern. Three distant riders
dwindling on a path away from the shore.
Tired, I reached for the oars.
I had never seen so many birds
on the lake. They were lifting, one by one
or dense in wedge-shaped flights.
It was quiet. There was only
my oars' creak-and-plash
and the soft rush of departing wings.

Safaddan

Many stories are told of Llyn Safaddan—Llangorse Lake—in Breconshire. The River Llyfni, which flows through it, is said never to mingle its waters with those of the lake. There are tales of a city buried under the lake. The birds of Safaddan sing only for the rightful heir to the throne of Wales. Giraldus says that three knights once put this tradition to the test. The two Anglo-Normans got no response to their commands, but for Gruffydd ap Rhys ap Tewdwr every bird cried aloud and beat its wings.

Through bruised reeds my boat thrust
into open water. First light broke thin mist
and was broken in a scatter of brightness
on the grey lake. In the depths
Llyfni coursed, eternally separate,
spurning the lake-waters beyond
intangible banks of its own force.
Silent lay the drowned city of legend
with its aqueous colonnades.

I had never seen the lake so thronged with birds
or known them so quiet. Hundreds there were,
out on the water, on the island,
and secret among the reeds.
On the further shore, three horsemen
rode to the lake's edge. Two dismounted,
each in turn shouting over the water—
I could not hear the words. From all
that intricate pattern of stilled wings
and watchful eyes, not one bird startled up.
The shouting sank dully into the lake.

Olchon Valley

June has lit such a summer fire;
such a fire in the hedges! Sober hazel-leaves,
tipped orange-pink, flare out of green,
burn translucent against the sun.

Once there was lit such a towering fire,
such a fire in the valley! Those who sat,
sober hearers, by hidden hearths, flared
out of homespun and leather, out of curbed flesh,
to spirit, to power, climbing and spreading—
flame the Word lit, words fanned.

Not a flame from that conflagration
breaks out here today, not a drift of its ashes
blurs the black slopes over the valley. But a fire
that was always here at the heart of quiet
gathers us into its congregation.

Black Mountains

To James and Stevie

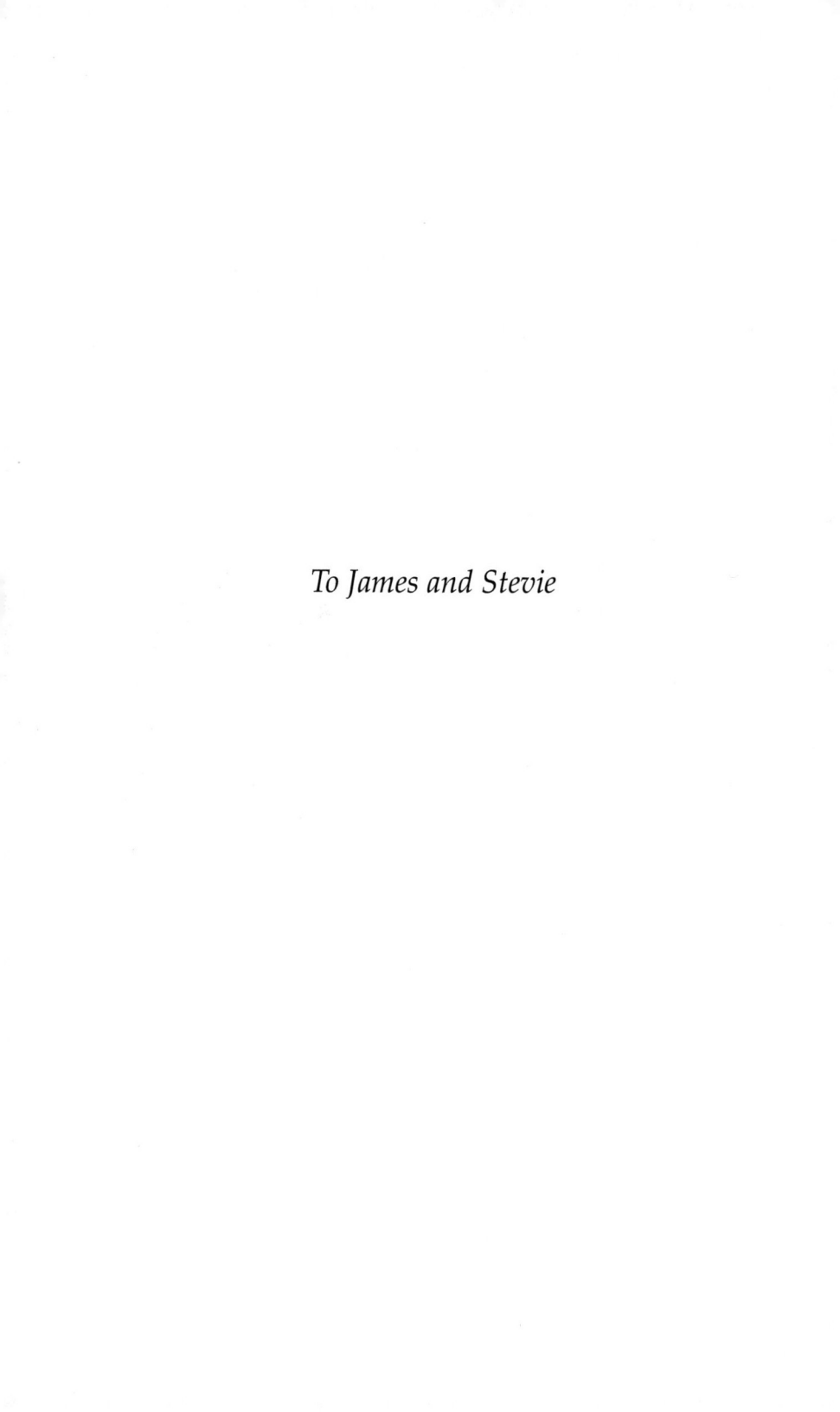

Foreword

I make no claim to know the Black Mountains well—only to remaining haunted by them after my visits to them, and to their outlying parishes. The area that inspired the poems is that covered by the end-paper map in Raymond Williams' *People of the Black Mountains*.

These poems have appeared scattered through some of my collections, but have not previously been grouped together.

Black Mountains:

The books in which they appeared are *Not Without Homage* (Christopher Davies), *The Print of Miracle* (Gomer), *The Fluent Moment, Singing to Wolves, New and Selected Poems* and *Time Being* (Seren) and *Above the Forests* (Cinnamon Press).

Contents

Foreword	3
Olchon Valley	7
Safaddan	8
Blaenllyfni Castle	10
The Fluent Moment	11
Singing to Wolves	
1. Llanthony	12
2. Capel y Ffîn	13
3. Cwmioie	14
4. Merthyr Clydawg	15
5. Michaelchurch Escley: Christ of the Trades	16
Angel and Invisible Tree	17
Angel with Wolf and Saint	18
Guérinou	
1. Patricio 2001	19
2. Tŷ'n-y-Llwyn	20
3. Incident in Vengeance Wood	22
4. New Houses	23
5. Macnamara's Mistress	24
6. The Hermitage	26
7. G.F.L.R.	28
Bridges	30
White Castle	32
Road to the Lake	33
Treachery	34
Capel-y-Ffîn Story	35
Garlanding the Urn	36
Time and the Running Child	37
Rights of Way	38
All Manner of Thing	39
Rainbow	40
At Capel-y-Ffîn	42
Sweetness	43
Tout Passe	44
Afterword: Matthew Jarvis	47

BLACK MOUNTAINS

RUTH BIDGOOD